Kids will love turning simple supplies into these 13 crafty creations.

I0893017

LEISURE ARTS, INC. • Maumelle, Arkansas

Wooden Clothespin Dolls

SHOPPING LIST

- ☐ $3^3/_4$" long round wooden clothespins
- ☐ chenille stems for arms
- ☐ brown acrylic paint and a paintbrush (optional)
- ☐ craft cord or embroidery floss (3 colors for clothes and 1 color for hair)
- ☐ two 10mm wooden beads for hands
- ☐ fine-point black permanent pen
- ☐ paper towels (optional)
- ☐ scissors
- ☐ craft glue

To make one Doll:

Steps that require an adult have this symbol.*

1. If you want your doll to have a dark skin tone, thin the brown paint with water. Brush the thinned paint on a clothespin; wipe it off with a paper towel.

*2. For the arms, cut a 5" length from the chenille stem. Place the center of the chenille stem between the clothespin's "legs." Bring one end to the front and up into place on one side for an arm. Bring the other end to the back and up into place for the other arm ***(Fig. 1)***.

Fig. 1

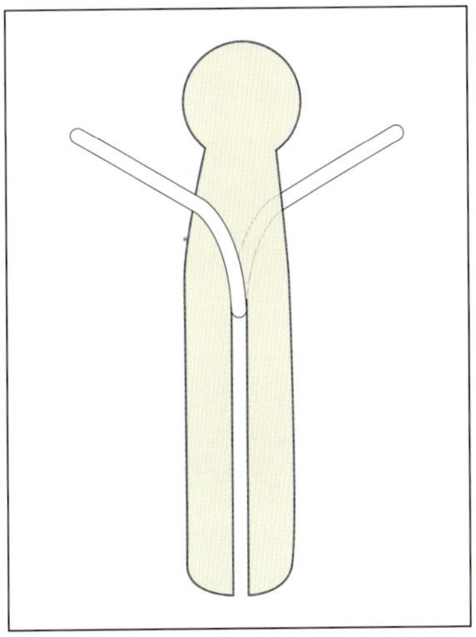

3. Wrap craft cord around the chenille stem and clothespin to make a top. End the thread on the back with a drop of glue. Wrap the cord around the clothespin to make a skirt ***(Fig. 2)***. Trim the ends of the chenille stems if needed and glue a bead to the end of each arm for hands.

Fig. 2

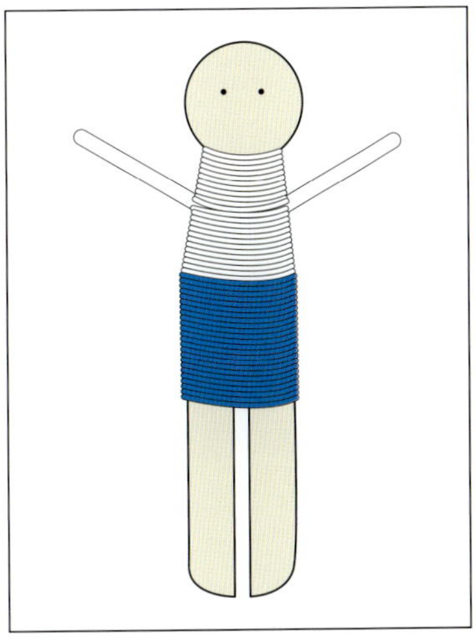

*4. For the hair, cut 40-50 3" long pieces of craft cord. Match the ends and stack all the pieces together. For the bow, cut 2 8" long pieces of craft cord. Tie the 8" pieces in a bow about 1" from 1 end of the hair ***(Fig. 3)***. Spreading all the shorter ends of the hair around the top of the clothespin, glue the hair to the clothespin. Trim the bangs and the hair as you like.

Fig. 3

5. Use the permanent pen to make dots for eyes on the clothespin.

*6. For the over skirt, cut a 12" piece of craft cord. Cut a total of 40 2" pieces of cord from 3 colors. Holding 2 pieces together as one, attach the short pieces to the 12" piece with Lark's Head knots, always pulling the knots tight ***(Fig. 4)***. Tie the over skirt around the doll's waist; trim the ends.

Fig. 4

*7. Make the pom-poms just like the hair using 1 1/2" pieces tied in the center with an 8" piece. Trim the pom-poms as you like; glue to the hands.

Silly Snow Globe

Designed by Monica Seagrave

SHOPPING LIST

- ☐ jar with tight fitting lid (we used a 16 oz mason jar with a self-sealing lid and separate ring)
- ☐ light corn syrup
- ☐ glitter
- ☐ two 2" x 2" photpgraphs
- ☐ small binder clip
- ☐ water
- ☐ laminating machine (or have photos laminated at an office supply store or copy shop)
- ☐ low-temp glue gun and glue sticks

To make the Snow Globe:

Steps that require an adult have this symbol.*

1. Take some silly photos of yourself or a friend, size to 2" x 2" on a computer and print; cut out. You could also make copies of photos you already have and trim the copies to the right size.

***2.** Place the photos back to back; laminate together. Allowing 1/4" of clear lamination on the top and side edges and 2" at the bottom, trim the laminated photo. Center and attach the binder clip to the bottom edge of the photo. Insert the photo in the jar to check the size; remove the photo and trim the laminated bottom and sides as needed to fit in the jar.

3. Securely glue the clip to the inside of the self sealing lid; allow glue to completely harden.

4. With the jar right side up, pour 1/4 cup of corn syrup into the jar. Leaving about 1/4" of room at the top, fill the jar with water; add a pinch or two of glitter. Place the lid on the jar and securely attach the ring.

***Tip:** Hold the jar over a sink when attaching the lid just in case the water overflows.*

Wooden Bookmarks

SHOPPING LIST

- ☐ jumbo crafts sticks
- ☐ acrylic paint (desired colors)
- ☐ paintbrush
- ☐ $1^{3}/_{8}$" high wood letters
- ☐ assorted beads
- ☐ craft cord or embroidery floss
- ☐ push pin
- ☐ scissors
- ☐ craft glue

To make one Bookmark:

Steps that require an adult have this symbol.*

1. Paint a craft stick and a wooden letter with colors you like.

*2. Wiggling the push pin from side to side and in a circular motion to enlarge the hole, punch a hole through one end of the craft stick.

3. Cut two 10" pieces of craft cord. Add a dab of glue to the end of one piece; twist the ends and allow to dry slightly. Repeat with the other piece. Insert the glued end of each piece through the hole. With the ends even, knot the cords at the end of the craft stick.

4. Leaving tails, knot the cords at the top of the letter. Slide a bead on two cord tails; knot ends. Repeat with remaining cord tails.

Pom-Pom Launcher & Pouch

SHOPPING LIST

- ☐ assorted pom-poms for "launching"
- ☐ assorted pom-poms to decorate pouch
- ☐ 9" x 12" felt sheets (1 solid color and 1 printed)
- ☐ assorted chenille stems
- ☐ disposable plastic cup with a 2" bottom diameter
- ☐ 12" round balloon
- ☐ duct tape
- ☐ 31" piece of paracord for strap
- ☐ craft knife
- ☐ craft glue
- ☐ stapler (optional)

To make the Launcher:

Steps that require an adult have this symbol.*

*1. Cut the cup about 2 1/2" from the bottom ***(Fig. 1)***. Cut a 1 1/4" diameter hole in the bottom of the cup ***(Fig. 2)***.

Fig. 1

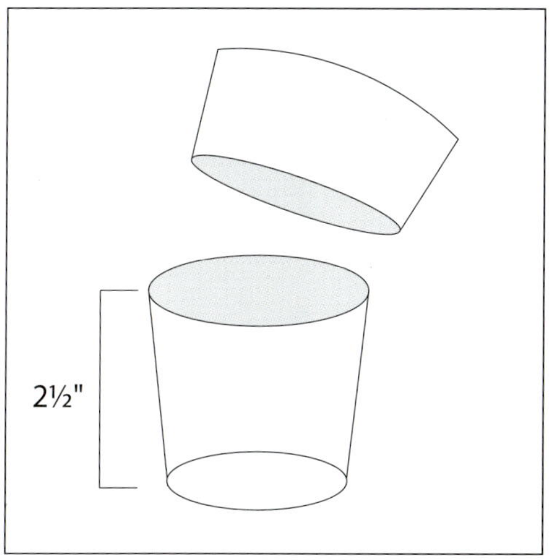

Fig. 2

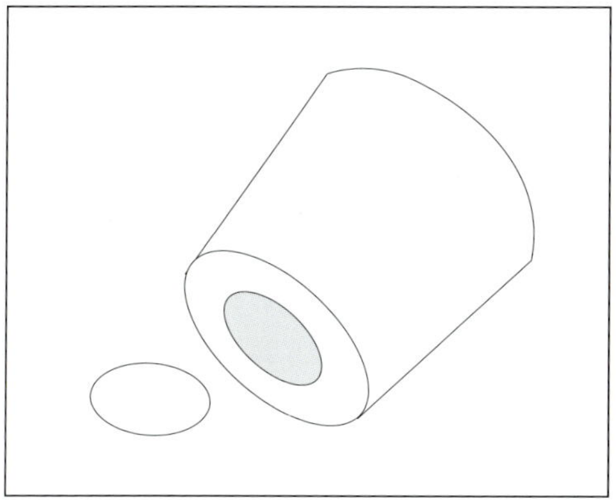

*2. Knot the balloon end. Cut the balloon about 4" from the knot. Stretch the balloon and slip it onto the cup, centering the knot under the hole. Securely tape the balloon to the cup.

3. Launch each pom-pom by dropping it into the launcher, pulling on the balloon knot, and letting go of the knot.

To make the Pouch:

*1. Matching short ends, fold the solid color felt sheet in half. Glue or staple the short sides together. Cut two 1 1/2" x 6" pieces of printed felt. Wrap and glue these pieces over the pouch side edges.

2. For the strap, fold each end of the paracord 1 1/2" toward the center. Leaving a loop, secure with duct tape .

*3. Cut a 3" piece of chenille stem. Thread it through one loop on the strap. Fold the chenille stem in half and securely glue to one inside corner of the pouch. Repeat with remaining end of the strap.

4. Shape chenille stems into a "P", "O" , and "W". Glue the letters and some pom-poms to the pouch front.

My Artwork Decoupage Plaque

SHOPPING LIST

- ☐ unfinished wood plaque (ours is about 9" x12")
- ☐ black chalkboard paint and foam paintbrush
- ☐ Mod Podge® Matte and paintbrush
- ☐ photocopy of artwork sized to fit plaque
- ☐ alphabet stickers
- ☐ fine-grit sandpaper
- ☐ squeegee, brayer, or rolling pin (optional)

Designed by Mary Sullivan Hutcheson

To make the Plaque:

Steps that require an adult have this symbol. Allow paint and Mod Podge to dry between applications.*

1. Sand plaque; wipe with a damp paper towel.
2. Paint plaque with 2 coats of chalkboard paint.
3. Apply one coat of Mod Podge to the front of the artwork; allow to dry. Trim artwork if needed.
4. Apply one coat of Mod Podge to the back of the artwork. While still wet, press the artwork onto the plaque; smooth from the center to the outer edges.

***Tip:** Using a squeegee, brayer, or rolling pin makes it easy to smooth the paper and get rid of any air bubbles under the paper.*

5. Apply stickers to spell the artist's name.
6. Apply one coat of Mod Podge over the entire plaque front to seal.

Wooden Snowflakes

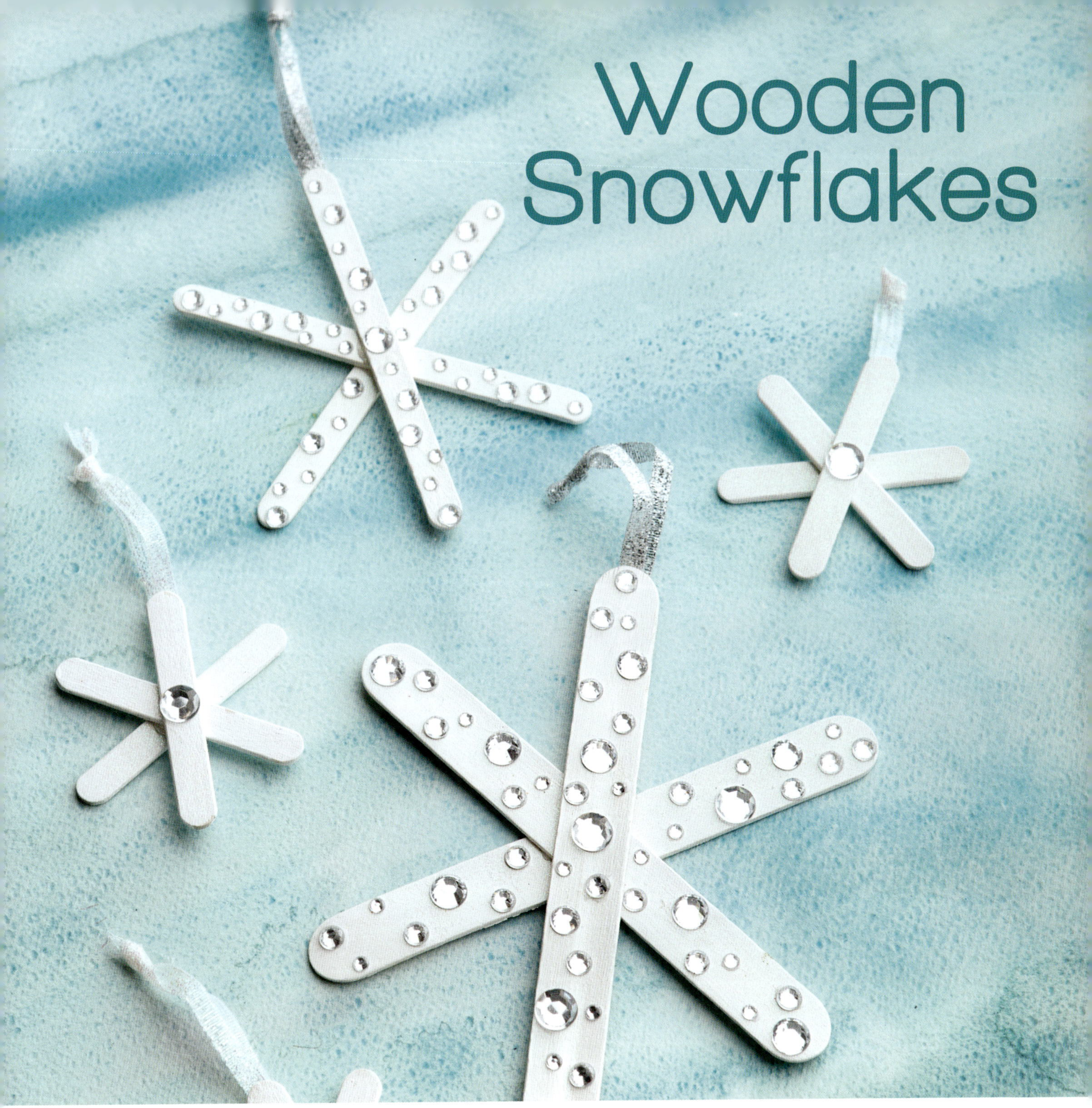

SHOPPING LIST

- ☐ craft sticks (we used jumbo, standard, and mini craft sticks)
- ☐ acrylic paint (white)
- ☐ acrylic glitter paint (silver)
- ☐ paintbrush
- ☐ assorted jewel stones
- ☐ 1/4" wide ribbon
- ☐ craft glue

To make one Snowflake:

1. Paint 3 same size craft sticks white; let dry. Paint the sticks again with glitter paint.
2. Stack and glue the sticks together.
3. Glue jewel stones to the snowflake.
4. Cut a 6" piece of ribbon. Fold the ribbon in half; knot the loose ends together. Glue the folded end to the snowflake.

Wooden Critters

Designed by Lora Puls

BASIC SUPPLIES

- ☐ scissors
- ☐ small and medium paintbrushes
- ☐ low-temp glue gun and glue sticks
- ☐ additional supplies are listed with each project

Steps that require and adult have this symbol. Always let the paint dry between steps.*

LIZARD

- ☐ 6" long jumbo craft stick
- ☐ 2" heart-shaped wood disc
- ☐ acrylic paint (green and red)
- ☐ wiggle eyes
- ☐ chenille stems (1 green, 1 red, and 2 black)

1. For the body and head, paint the stick and the heart green. Use the handle of a paint brush dipped in red paint to make dots for the nose.

***2.** From 2 black chenille stems, cut 2 7$\frac{1}{2}$" body stripes/rear legs. For the front legs, you will use 1 of the leftover black 4$\frac{1}{2}$" pieces. From the red chenille stem, cut 1 3" eyebrow.

***3.** Glue the green chenille stem in the center of the craft stick; bend and curl the excess into a tail. Glue one black body stripe/rear leg on either side of the green stick; bend the excess into legs. Glue the front leg piece under the body about 2" from the end; bend to make the legs.

***4.** Bend and glue the eyebrow piece around the top of the head; glue the eyes just below the eyebrows. Glue the head to the body.

BUG

- ☐ 2$\frac{1}{2}$" round wood disc
- ☐ 1$\frac{1}{4}$" round wood disc
- ☐ acrylic paint (black, green, hot pink, and neon yellow)
- ☐ wiggle eyes
- ☐ 2 neon yellow pom-poms
- ☐ chenille stems (1 black and 3 hot pink)

1. For the body, paint the large disc neon yellow and green. Paint the detail lines black. Use a pencil eraser dipped in green paint to make the large spots; allow to dry. Repeat to make hot pink spots on top of the green. Use the handle of a paint brush dipped in hot pink paint to make the small spots. For the head, paint the small disc black.

***2.** From the black chenille stem, cut 2 1$\frac{1}{2}$" antennae. Bend and glue the antennae to the head. Glue the eyes to the pom-poms. Glue the pom-poms to the head over the antennae ends. Glue the head to the body.

***3.** Using a whole pink chenille stem for each set of legs, bend and glue the legs under the body.

CATERPILLAR

- ☐ 4$\frac{1}{2}$" long standard craft stick
- ☐ acrylic paint (green)
- ☐ wiggle eyes
- ☐ chenille stems (2 black and 1 blue)
- ☐ 6 green pom-poms
- ☐ 3 light green pom-poms

1. For the body, paint the stick green.

***2.** From the black chenille stems, cut 8 2" legs. From the blue chenille stem, cut 1 2" antennae.

***3.** Beginning with a light green pom-pom for the head, glue the pom-poms to the craft stick. Glue the eyes to the head.

***4.** Bend and glue the legs over the body between each pom-pom. Fold the antennae in half; glue in place behind the head.

LADYBUG

- ☐ $3^1/_2$" oval wood disc
- ☐ $1^1/_4$" round wood disc
- ☐ acrylic paint (black and red)
- ☐ wiggle eyes
- ☐ chenille stems (black)

1. For the body, paint the oval disc red and black. Use the handle of a paint brush dipped in black paint to make the spots. For the head, paint the round disc black.

*2. From the chenille stem, cut 6 4" legs and 2 $1^1/_2$" antennae.

*3. Bend and glue the legs under the body. Bend and glue the antennae under the head. Glue the eyes to the head, then glue the head to the body.

TURTLE

- ☐ $3^1/_2$" oval wood disc
- ☐ $1^1/_4$" round wood disc
- ☐ $^3/_4$" round wood disc
- ☐ acrylic paint (green and light green)
- ☐ wiggle eyes
- ☐ chenille stem (green)
- ☐ 2 pink pom-poms

1. For the body, paint the oval light green with green spots. For the head and feet, paint all the wood rounds green. Paint a light green mouth and 2 dots for the nose on the head.

*2. Glue the feet under the body. Glue the head to the body. Glue the pom-poms to the head; Glue the eyes to the pom-poms.

*3. For the tail, cut a 2" piece from the chenille stem. Fold the piece in half; glue the tail to the body.

OCTOPUS

- ☐ $3^3/_4$" 8-petal wood disc
- ☐ acrylic paint (purple)
- ☐ acrylic glitter paint (purple)
- ☐ wiggle eyes
- ☐ very large lavender pom-pom

1. Paint the wood shape purple. When dry, apply a coat of purple glitter paint.

*2. Glue the pom-pom to the body then glue the eyes to the pom-pom.

DRAGONFLY

- ☐ $4^1/_2$" long standard craft stick
- ☐ 2 2" oval wood discs
- ☐ 2 $1^1/_2$" oval wood discs
- ☐ acrylic paint (purple and white)
- ☐ acrylic glitter paint (purple and white)
- ☐ wiggle eyes
- ☐ 3 purple pom-poms

1. For the body, paint the craft stick purple. When dry, apply a coat of purple glitter paint.

2. For the wings, paint the ovals white. When dry, apply a coat of white glitter paint. Use the handle of a paint brush dipped in purple glitter paint to add dots to the wings.

*3. Glue the wings under the body. Glue the eyes and pom-poms to the body

Sheep & Lion Marionettes

SHOPPING LIST

For each animal:

- ☐ 2 toilet paper tubes
- ☐ light-weight cotton cord
- ☐ 2 jumbo craft sticks
- ☐ 2 wiggle eyes
- ☐ fine-point black permanent marker
- ☐ tracing paper
- ☐ scissors
- ☐ 1/4" hole punch
- ☐ low-temp glue gun and glue sticks

For the sheep:

- ☐ large white pom-poms
- ☐ small black pom-poms
- ☐ heavy-weight scrapbook paper (white and black)
- ☐ 8 white pony beads
- ☐ 48 black pony beads

For the lion:

- ☐ large dark yellow and gold pom-poms
- ☐ small gold pom-poms
- ☐ heavy-weight scrapbook paper (brown and tan)
- ☐ 62 brown pony beads

***Tip:** Tightly wrap a small piece of tape around the cut cord ends to make it easier to thread the cord through the punched holes and the beads.*

Designed by Monica Seagrave

To make the Sheep:

Adult supervision is reccomended for this project.

1. For the head, cut one tube in half. The remaining whole tube is the body. Refer to **Fig. 1** to punch 4 holes in the head and **Fig. 2** to punch 6 holes in the body for the strings.

2. For the back legs, tie a black bead on one end of a 12" cord length. Thread 11 more beads on the cord. Thread the cord through one leg hole at the back of the body, through the body and out the opposite hole. Thread 12 beads on the cord. Keeping the beads close to the body, tie the cord around the last bead ***(Fig. 3)***. Repeat to add the front legs.

3. Making sure not to block any of the punched holes and using glue to attach, completely cover the body and head with white pom-poms.

4. For the head control cords, tie a white bead to one end of an 18" cord length. With the bead inside the head, thread the cord through one side hole in the head. Repeat for remaining side hole.

5. For the face, trace the face, ear and forehead patterns, page 20, onto tracing paper; cut out. Use the patterns to cut a face from white scrapbook paper and 2 ears and the forehead from black scrapbook paper. Glue black pom-poms to the forehead. Glue the eyes to the face and the ears behind the face. Use the marker to draw a nose and mouth below the eyes. Glue the face to the head on the end closest to the 2 side head cords.

6. To assemble the head and body, tie an 18" cord through the neck hole in the top of the body. Thread 6 white beads on the cord. Thread the cord through the neck hole in the bottom and the control hole in the top of the head. Keeping the beads and cord taut, tie a knot close to the top hole.

7. Tie an 18" cord through the tail control hole in the top of the body.

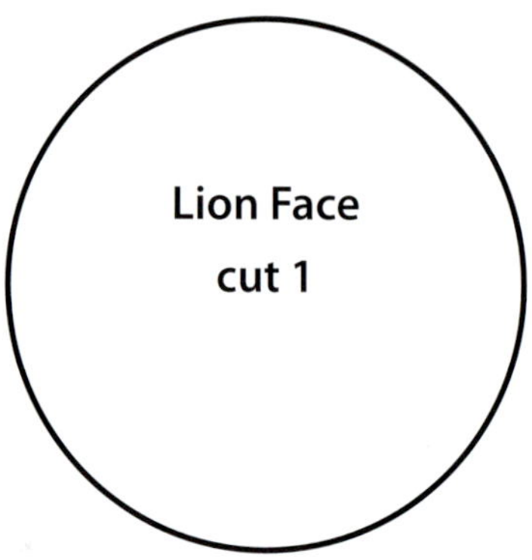

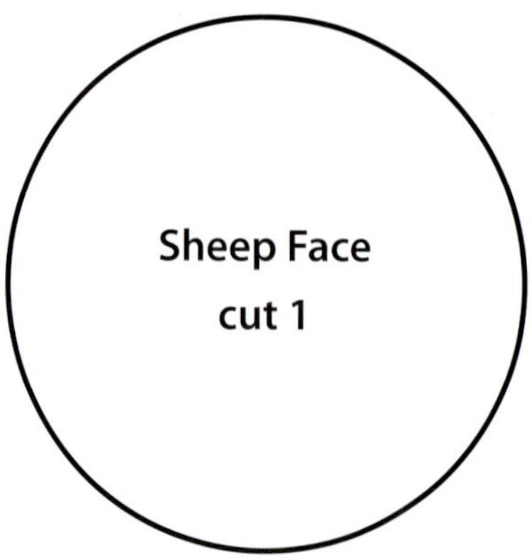

Fig. 1

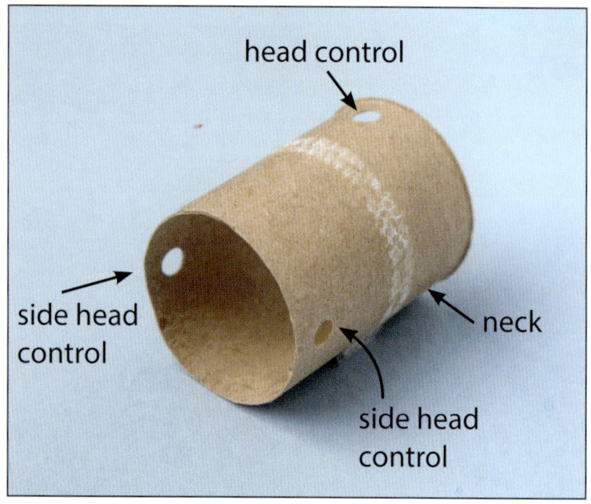

Fig. 2

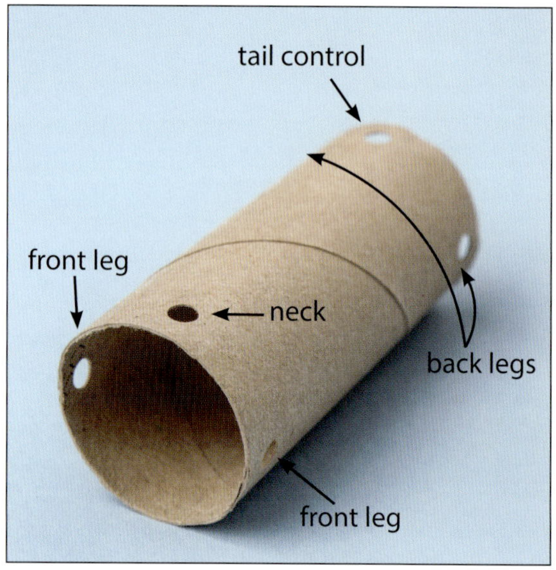

Fig. 3

8. To make the control bar, glue the 2 craft sticks together in a "t "shape ***(Fig. 4)***. Glue the neck cord to the control bar just in front of the cross bar and the tail cord to the opposite end of the same bar. Glue one side head cord to each end of the cross bar. Wrap each cord around the control bar until you are happy with the length and the balance of the sheep; tape the cords in place on the control bar. ***Note:*** Taping the cords allows you to adjust the length and balance as you play with your marionette.

Fig. 4

9. Put a drop of glue on each knot and allow to harden; trim the cord ends.

To make the Lion:

Adult supervision is reccomended for this project.

1. Using brown beads, large dark yellow and gold pom-poms to cover the body and small gold pom-poms to cover the head, follow Steps 1-4 of Sheep.
2. For the face, trace the face, small mane, and large mane patterns onto tracing paper; cut out. Use the patterns to cut a face from tan scrapbook paper and the large and small manes from brown scrapbook paper. Make 1/4" deep, closely spaced cuts all around the edges of both the large and small manes. Layer and glue the large mane, small mane, and face. Glue the eyes to the face. Use the marker to draw a nose, mouth and whiskers below the eyes. Glue the face to the head on the end closest to the 2 side head cords.
3. Using brown beads, follow Step 6 of Sheep.
4. To make the tail and attach the rear cord, tie a brown bead to one end of an 18" cord. Thread 7 more beads on the cord. Thread the cord through the tail hole in the top of the body. Keeping the beads and cord taut, tie a knot close to the top hole. Glue a pom-pom to the end of the tail.
5. Follow Steps 8-9 of Sheep.

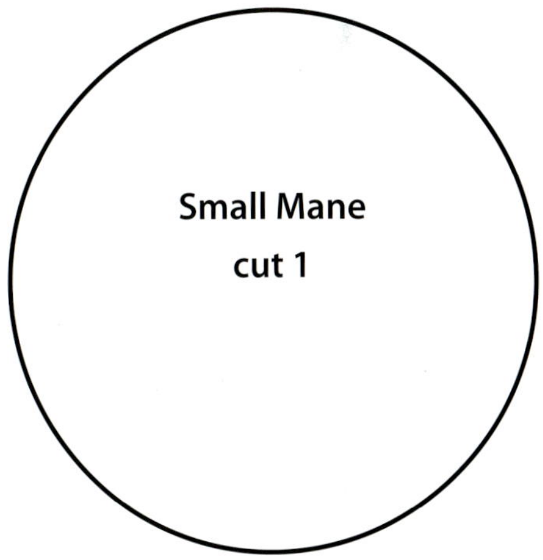

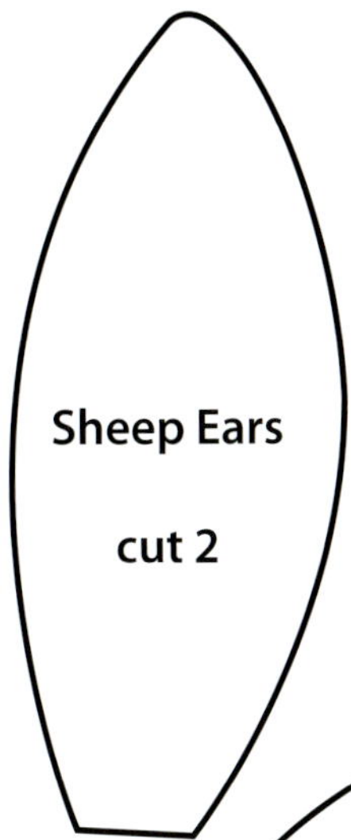

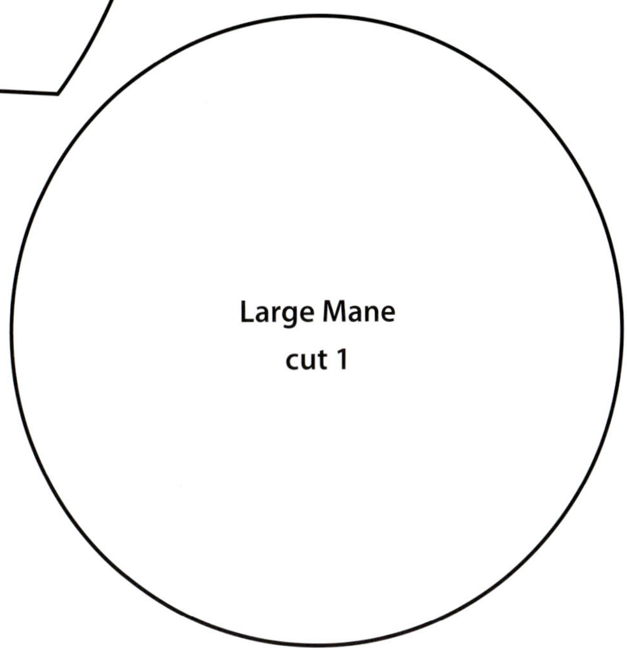

Yarn Wrapped Jar

Designed by Kelly Reider

SHOPPING LIST

- ☐ variegated medium weight yarn (approximately 60 yards)
- ☐ jar or bottle (our jar is 4 1/2" high but you can use any size or shape)
- ☐ double-sided tape
- ☐ 3" x 2" piece of cardboard
- ☐ scissors
- ☐ low-temp glue gun and glue sticks

To cover the Bottle:

1. Place a tape strip vertically on the jar from the neck to the bottom at the front and back of the jar. This will help hold the yarn in place as you wrap.

*2. Pressing the yarn into the tape, start at the bottom back to tightly wrap the yarn around the jar. Use a drop of glue to secure the yarn to the jar. Continue wrapping, securing the yarn with glue as needed, until you reach the top.

*3. Working from the top to the bottom, wrap the jar a second time, filling in any uncovered areas with yarn. When you reach the bottom, cut the yarn and secure the yarn end with glue.

4. To make the pom-pom, wind the yarn around the cardboard about 50 times – the more you wind, the fluffier the pom-pom ***(Fig. 1)***.

Fig. 1

*5. Carefully slip the yarn off the cardboard and firmly tie an 18" piece of yarn around the middle ***(Fig. 2)***; leave the yarn tails long enough to tie around the jar. Cut the loops on each end of the pom-pom ***(Fig. 3)*** and trim into a ball.

Fig. 2

Fig. 3

6. Knot the yarn tails together about 1" away from the pom-pom. Tie the tails around the jar neck and secure with a drop of glue; trim the tails.

Tip: *Fill your jar with sand or rice and add a large artifical flower.*

Fingerprint Pot & Muffin Cup Flowers

Designed by Monica Seagrave

SHOPPING LIST

- ☐ 6" clay pot
- ☐ 8-10 assorted colors of acrylic paint
- ☐ 1" wide paintbrush
- ☐ small round paintbrush for details
- ☐ green scrapbook paper for leaves
- ☐ 4 white standard paper baking cups
- ☐ 4 white mini paper baking cups
- ☐ green print paper drinking straws
- ☐ acrylic jewels (about 3/4" or 19 mm diameter)
- ☐ assorted markers to color flowers
- ☐ fine-point black permanent marker
- ☐ tracing paper
- ☐ scissors
- ☐ small foam plates
- ☐ rice or sand
- ☐ low-temp glue gun and glue sticks
- ☐ duct or masking tape

To make the Flowerpot:

Steps that require an adult have this symbol. Always allow paint to dry between applications.*

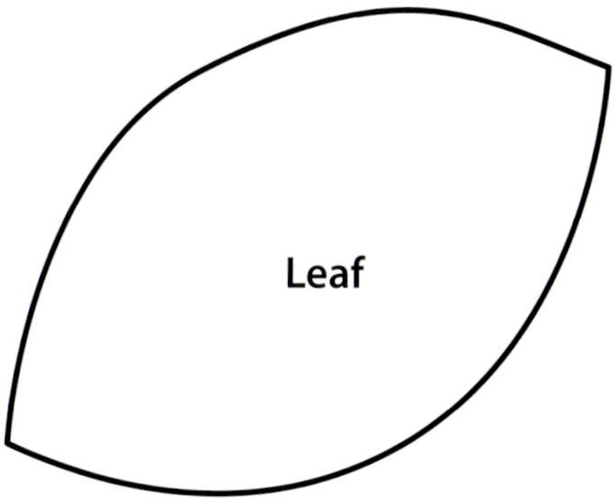

1. Use the large brush to paint the inside and outside of the rim with 2 coats of aqua.

2. Pour a small amount of several different paint colors onto foam plates. Use your thumb and fingers to make different sizes and colors of fingerprints on the pot. Use the black fine-point marker and small round paintbrush to add details like legs and eyes to the fingerprints. ***Note:*** Suggestions for turning fingerprints into critters include frogs, bees, flowers, snails, caterpillars, spiders, and cats.

3. Completely cover the hole in the bottom of the pot with tape. Fill the pot with rice or sand.

4. For each flower, use the assorted markers to color the baking cup liners as desired; allow to dry. Glue a mini liner to the center of a standard liner; glue a jewel in the center of the flower.

***5.** Trace the leaf pattern onto tracing paper; cut out. Draw around the pattern on the scrapbook paper. Cut out and make small cuts (about 1/8" apart and 1/8" deep) around the edges of the leaf to make fringed edges.

***6.** Glue a flower to one end of each straw; attach a leaf to the stem below the flower.

7. Arrange the flowers in the pot.

Designed by
Monica Seagrave

Tin Can Peacock Windsock

SHOPPING LIST

- ☐ 20 oz tin can
- ☐ royal blue acrylic paint and a paintbrush
- ☐ 60" each of 3 different ribbons/trims (we used jumbo rickrack, fold-over elastic, and a sequin trim)
- ☐ aqua and purple feathers
- ☐ glitter chenille stems (2 blue and 1 each of purple and green)
- ☐ 2 wiggle eyes
- ☐ orange construction paper
- ☐ 5" x 1" piece of royal blue craft foam
- ☐ 12" piece of jute
- ☐ medium-grit sandpaper
- ☐ tracing paper
- ☐ scissors
- ☐ low-temp glue gun and glue sticks

To make the Windsock:

Adult supervision is reccomended for this project.. Always allow paint and glue to dry between applications.

1. Use a can opener to remove both ends from the can; use the sand paper to smooth away sharp edges if needed. Wash, rinse, and dry the can.
2. Lightly sand the outside of the can; wipe with a damp paper towel and let dry.
3. Paint the can blue. Apply1-2 additional coats of paint, if needed.
4. For the streamers, cut three 20" pieces from each ribbon/trim. Spacing evenly and alternating the ribbon/trims, glue the streamers inside one edge of the can. This end is the bottom of the windsock.
5. Cut a 9" piece from each color of glitter chenille stems; bend each piece into a teardrop shape and twist the ends to secure. Cut three 4" pieces from the remaining blue glitter chenille stem.

6. Arrange and glue 5 feathers in a fan shape on the craft foam. Glue the 3 chenille stem teardrops over the feathers. Glue one or two small feathers over the chenille stem ends.

7. Glue the feathered foam piece just inside the top edge of the can. Glue the three 4" chenille stem pieces to the inside edge of the can, opposite the feathers. Bend the free end of each piece under $^{1}/_{4}$" and curl the pieces over the can edge.

8. Trace the beak pattern onto tracing paper; cut out. Draw around the beak pattern on the orange construction paper; cut out. Fold the beak in half. Glue the beak to the front of the can, about $1^{3}/_{4}$" below the top edge and centered under the 3 curled chenille stem pieces.

9. Glue the wiggly eyes to the can front just above the beak.

10. On opposite sides, glue about $^{1}/_{2}$" of each jute end to the inside top edge of the can for a hanger.

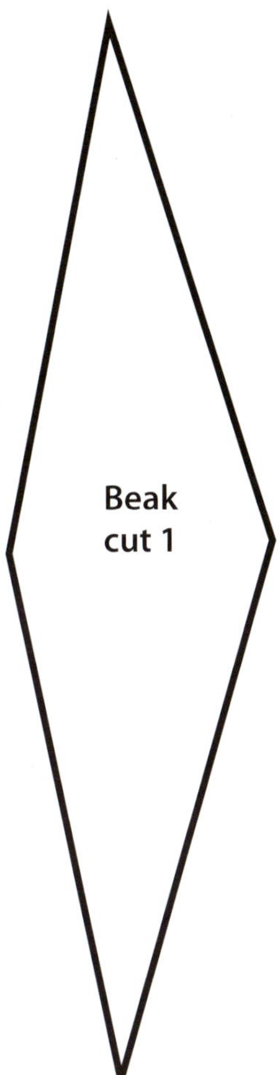

Paper Tube Sneaky Snake

SHOPPING LIST

- ☐ 3 toilet paper tubes
- ☐ three 36" pieces of light-weight cotton cord
- ☐ green acrylic paint and a paintbrush
- ☐ 3" x 3" piece of white craft foam
- ☐ 2 wiggle eyes
- ☐ 1/2" x 2" piece of red felt for the tongue
- ☐ 1 1/2" long plastic egg
- ☐ assorted markers (we used blue, pink, purple, and yellow)
- ☐ 1/4" hole punch
- ☐ tracing paper
- ☐ scissors
- ☐ stapler
- ☐ craft glue

Designed by
Monica Seagrave

To make the Snake:

Steps that require an adult have this symbol.*

*1. Cut each paper tube in half. Slightly flatten one half tube; cut one end into a point ***(Figs. 1-2)***.

Fig. 1

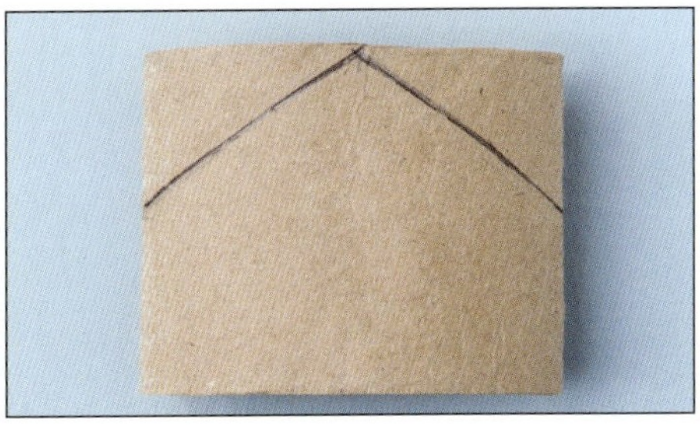

Fig. 2

*2. Refer to **Fig 3** to punch 2 holes in each side of 4 half tubes. Punch 1 hole in each side of 1 half tube (head) and the pointed tube (tail).

Fig. 3

3. Paint all of the tube pieces green and allow to dry.

4. Arrange the tube pieces as shown in **Assembly Diagram**. Tie one cord piece through one tail hole. Thread the cord in and out of the tube holes on one side of the snake. Knot the cord after going through the head hole **(Fig. 4)**. Repeat using a second cord piece on the opposite side of the snake. Put a drop of glue on each knot and allow to dry; trim the cord tails close to the knots.

Assembly Diagram

Fig. 4

5. Tape the egg to the remaining cord piece, then thread the cord through the snake from front to back. Trim the cord to about 20" and knot the end. Flatten and staple the sides of the tail together ***(Fig. 5)***.

Fig. 5

*6. Cut a "V" in one end of the tongue; glue the tongue inside the head. Glue the eyes to the top of the head.

*7. Trace the diamond pattern onto tracing paper; cut out. Use the pattern to draw 4 diamonds on the craft foam; cut out. Use the markers to color the diamonds. Glue one diamond to each body section.

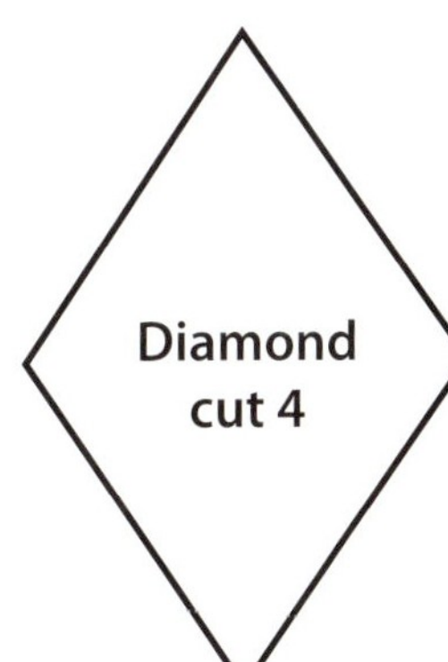

Wooden Airplanes

SHOPPING LIST

- ☐ wooden spring type clothespins
- ☐ standard craft sticks and mini craft sticks
- ☐ acrylic paint (red, blue, yellow, and green)
- ☐ paintbrush
- ☐ scissors
- ☐ craft glue

To make one Airplane:

Steps that require an adult have this symbol.*

*1. Cut a teardrop shape from one end of 1 mini craft stick.

2. Paint the clothespin red. Paint 2 standard craft sticks blue. Paint 1 mini craft stick yellow. Paint the teardrop shape green.

3. Glue 1 blue stick on the top and bottom of the red clothespin. Glue the yellow stick on top pf the clothespin near the end. Glue the teardrop shape to the yellow stick.

Production Team: Technical Writer - Jean Lewis; Technical Associate - Mary Sullivan Hutcheson; Editorial Writer - Susan Frantz Wiles; Senior Graphic Artist - Lora Puls; Graphic Artist - Kellie McAnulty; Photo Stylist - Stephanie Moore; and Photographer - Jason Masters.